United States Government Accountability Office

Report to Congressional Committees

I0448467

September 2013

FAA FACILITIES

Improved Condition Assessment Methods Could Better Inform Maintenance Decisions and Capital-Planning Efforts

September 2013

GAO Highlights

Highlights of GAO-13-757, a report to Congressional Committees

FAA FACILITIES

Improved Condition Assessment Methods Could Better Inform Maintenance Decisions and Capital-Planning Efforts

Why GAO Did This Study

Of the approximately 1,230 facilities that FAA staff occupy, FAA is responsible for maintaining over 40 percent of them—spending over $1 billion since 2008; most of the remaining facilities are leased and maintained by the lessors. Yet, according to FAA officials, air traffic control facilities—the bulk of FAA-maintained facilities—have a current maintenance backlog of about $259 million. Deferring maintenance on facilities could compromise safe airspace operations.

The FAA Modernization and Reform Act of 2012 mandated that GAO study the condition of FAA-staffed facilities. This report addresses, among other things, (1) the condition of FAA-staffed facilities and the reliability of assessment methods; (2) the extent to which FAA has responded to identified safety deficiencies; and (3) the extent to which FAA's actions to ensure that its facilities are in good condition follow leading practices. GAO analyzed data and documents from FAA, the Department of Labor, and GSA, and interviewed agency officials and others, including union representatives.

What GAO Recommends

To ensure more accurate and reliable data to help decision making on its facilities' conditions, GAO is recommending that FAA (1) improve the precision of the methods used to estimate the conditions of uninspected terminal facilities and (2) implement a plan to improve REMS, consistent with sound data collection practices. DOT provided technical comments, which we incorporated as appropriate.

View GAO-13-757. For more information, contact Gerald Dillingham, 202-512-2834, dillinghamg@gao.gov

What GAO Found

According to data provided by FAA and the General Services Administration (GSA), federally maintained facilities FAA occupies are generally in fair to good condition. FAA assesses the condition of staffed facilities in several ways, including direct inspections. However, the condition of approximately 75 percent of Air Traffic Organization's (ATO) terminal facilities is based on estimates derived from the approximately 25 percent of facilities that have been inspected over the last 6 years. Our analysis of FAA's statistical model for estimating the condition of uninspected terminal facilities found it to be imprecise; it uses one variable—age of the facility—to estimate the facility's condition. Adding other variables that are correlated with condition, such as facility replacement value and use, could potentially improve the estimate's accuracy. In addition, facility condition data in FAA's Real Estate Management System (REMS)—FAA's database for tracking its inventory of real property assets, including the size, replacement value, and condition of each asset—are not derived from sound data collection practices and did not match facility condition data from ATO or other FAA organizational components responsible for maintaining these facilities. Inaccuracies in REMS data undermine its usefulness as a management tool.

Entities Responsible for Maintaining FAA's Staffed Facilities, 2013

Facility description	FAA	GSA	Other (incl. non-federal	Total
Operations (terminal & en-route facilities)	425	--	137	562
Administrative, technical, training	80	8	583	671
Total	505	8	720	1233

Source: GAO analysis of FAA and GSA data.

FAA has mechanisms to identify and mitigate safety deficiencies at FAA facilities. For example, FAA annually conducts a safety and health inspection, as required by regulation, at each of its staffed facilities under its Environmental and Occupational Safety and Health program. Identified deficiencies are tracked to ensure they are mitigated. FAA also established safety committees to maintain an open channel of communication between employees and managers concerning safety matters in the workplace. FAA employees may also report any hazards they identify to FAA managers at their facility or, as applicable, to their union representative or the Occupational Safety and Health Administration.

FAA has taken actions to strengthen its capital planning process to help ensure its facilities are in good condition. In 2012, FAA created a Facilities Group Manager position within ATO to coordinate management of all its operations facilities, both staffed and unstaffed. ATO's Facilities Group Manager is taking steps to develop a standard prioritization process focusing on safety, mission critical needs, and environmental requirements to modernize and sustain existing equipment, facilities, and services; this approach is to be used to develop FAA's future budget requests. FAA is developing a 10-year "Get Well" plan that, among other things, is to establish an approach to reduce the maintenance backlog for existing facilities. This plan, along with a facilities consolidation report the agency is developing in response to the FAA Modernization and Reform Act of 2012, should help provide justification and cost projections for maintaining facilities in good condition.

_____ United States Government Accountability Office

Contents

Figures

GAO U.S. GOVERNMENT ACCOUNTABILITY OFFICE

441 G St. N.W.
Washington, DC 20548

September 10, 2013

The Honorable John D. Rockefeller IV
Chairman
The Honorable John Thune
Ranking Member
Committee on Commerce, Science, and Transportation
United States Senate

The Honorable Bill Shuster
Chairman
The Honorable Nick J. Rahall, II
Ranking Member
Committee on Transportation and Infrastructure
House of Representatives

For the Federal Aviation Administration (FAA) to safely operate the most complex airspace system in the world, its employees and systems need to be housed in facilities that are in good and safe condition. FAA staff occupy approximately 1,230 facilities that serve administrative and operational functions. FAA is responsible for maintaining almost half of these facilities—primarily those used for air traffic control operations. The General Services Administration (GSA) maintains the federally owned facilities that FAA occupies for administrative purposes. As for the remaining facilities, FAA occupies them under leases or other agreements whereby the owner provides facility maintenance.

Since 2008, FAA has spent over $1 billion for repairs and improvements to the facilities it maintains. While some of the facilities that FAA maintains will become excess as a result of planned consolidation, most will likely remain in service to support FAA's mission. To sustain these facilities, FAA officials require accurate information about facility condition to plan and prioritize maintenance and repairs so that operational needs can be met in a safe working environment. FAA's efforts to address the needs of its aging facilities portfolio, meet facilities requirements related to implementation of the Next Generation Air Transportation System (NextGen),[1] and move forward with facility consolidation plans will likely

---

[1] NextGen is a complex undertaking that requires acquiring new integrated air traffic control systems; developing new flight procedures, standards, and regulations; and creating and maintaining supporting infrastructure to create a more automated aircraft-centered, satellite-based air transportation system.

be affected by resource constraints as a result of expected lower future budgets. The challenges presented by these circumstances relate to long-standing problems that we have identified with federal real property, an area that we have designated as high-risk.[2]

Congress mandated in the FAA Modernization and Reform Act of 2012 that we study the condition of FAA-staffed facilities, including administrative and operational facilities, employee occupational safety and health issues, and resources allocated to facility maintenance and renovation.[3] This report follows up an interim report we issued on May 9, 2013, which discussed our preliminary findings.[4] To meet the mandate, this report addresses the following questions:

1. What is known about the conditions of FAA-staffed facilities and to what extent are the assessment methods and resulting data reliable?

2. What have been the workplace injuries and illnesses reported by FAA employees in workers' compensation claims, and to what extent has FAA met its targets for processing claims?

3. To what extent has FAA responded to safety deficiencies identified through its inspections and those conducted by the Occupational Safety and Health Administration (OSHA)?

4. To what extent are actions FAA has taken to ensure that its facilities are in good condition, if any, consistent with leading practices for capital-investment decisions?

To determine what is known about the conditions of FAA facilities and the extent to which the methods used to make those determinations and the resulting data are reliable, we collected condition data from 2010 through

---

[2] GAO, *High-Risk Series: Federal Real Property*, GAO-03-122 (Washington, D.C.: January 2003) and GAO, *High-Risk Series: An Update*, GAO-13-283 (Washington, D.C.: February 2013). Our high-risk series identifies areas at high risk because of their greater vulnerabilities to waste, fraud, abuse, and mismanagement or major challenges associated with their economy, efficiency, or effectiveness. We identified federal real property as a high-risk area because of long-standing problems with excess and underutilized real property, deteriorating facilities, unreliable real property data, and costly space challenges shared by several agencies.

[3] FAA Modernization and Reform Act of 2012, Pub. L. No. 112-95, § 610, 126 Stat. 11, 117 (Feb. 14, 2012).

[4] GAO, *Preliminary Results of Work on FAA Facility Conditions and Workplace Safety*, GAO-13-509R (Washington, D.C.: May 9, 2013).

GAO-13-757 Facilities Condition

2012 from FAA and GSA. To assess the reliability of the FAA data we reviewed existing documentation, interviewed cognizant agency officials, and performed electronic testing for obvious errors in accuracy and completeness. To assess the reliability of the GSA data, we reviewed existing documentation and interviewed knowledgeable agency officials. We found that data in FAA's agency-wide Real Estate Management System (REMS) were not sufficiently reliable for describing facility condition, as discussed later in this report. However, we determined that data from other sources maintained by FAA organizational components with facilities maintenance responsibilities and from GSA were sufficiently reliable for this purpose. To determine whether the inspection methods used by FAA or GSA to obtain facility condition information were reliable for this purpose, we compared those methods with generally accepted industry standards and interviewed FAA and GSA facility officials and FAA's engineering consultants. We also interviewed FAA and union officials representing major aviation employee groups about facility conditions. To observe conditions and speak with knowledgeable staff to learn about any facility deficiencies and the projects for fixing them, we visited facilities supporting operations and administrative functions in each of FAA's three geographic service areas.[5] To determine the most common types of workplace injuries and illnesses FAA employees have reported, if any, we reviewed FAA and Department of Labor (Labor) workers' compensation data from 2007 through 2012. To determine the extent to which FAA has complied with its targets for processing claims, we compared actual performance to the targets. To assess the reliability of the data, we reviewed existing documentation, interviewed knowledgeable agency officials, and performed electronic testing for obvious errors in accuracy and completeness. We found the data to be sufficiently reliable for the purposes of this report. Because of the variability of factors that may contribute to reported injuries and illnesses, our study does not attempt to link workers' compensation claims to facility conditions. To determine how FAA has responded to any safety deficiencies identified through inspections of its facilities, we reviewed FAA and OSHA inspection reports and documents pertaining to how FAA has addressed deficiencies. Regarding actions FAA has taken to ensure that its facilities are in good and safe condition, consistent with leading practices, we reviewed FAA's process for making capital decisions and compared it to our and the Office of Management and Budget's (OMB)

---

[5] FAA's service areas comprise the eastern, central, and western regions of the country.

GAO-13-757 Facilities Condition

leading practices.[6] Appendix I has a more detailed discussion of our scope and methodology.

We conducted this performance audit from July 2012 to September 2013 in accordance with generally accepted government auditing standards. Those standards require that we plan and perform the audit to obtain sufficient, appropriate evidence to provide a reasonable basis for our findings and conclusions based on our audit objectives. We believe that the evidence we obtained provides a reasonable basis for our findings and conclusions based on our audit objectives.

Background

Facility Maintenance Responsibility

Responsibility for maintaining the approximately 1,230 staffed FAA facilities—ranging from administrative buildings to operations buildings such as air traffic control towers—is distributed among FAA, GSA, and other entities, as shown in table 1.[7] Within FAA, several components hold responsibility for facilities maintenance, including the Air Traffic Organization (ATO), Mike Monroney Aeronautical Center (Aeronautical Center), and William J. Hughes Technical Center (Technical Center). ATO maintains facilities supporting air traffic control operations at multiple locations across the country and overseas. These include en-route traffic control facilities that control high-altitude air traffic and terminal facilities that control low altitude air traffic. FAA's Aeronautical Center and Technical Center maintain facilities on their respective campuses in Oklahoma City and Atlantic City that provide research and training functions. GSA maintains some of FAA's administrative facilities including FAA's headquarters in Washington, D.C., and regional offices around the country. FAA also occupies several hundred facilities across the country

---

[6] GAO, *Executive Guide: Leading Practices in Capital Decision-Making.* GAO/AIMD-99-32 (Washington, D.C.: December 1998); OMB, *Capital Programming Guide,* Supplement to Office of Management and Budget Circular A-11: Planning, Budgeting, and Acquisition of Capital Assets (July 2012).

[7] The FAA Unstaffed Infrastructure Sustainment program manages approximately 30,000 unstaffed facilities that house, protect, and support National Airspace System (NAS) communications, navigation, surveillance, weather, and other air traffic control equipment. This study is limited to FAA-staffed facilities maintained by FAA and GSA. For more information on unstaffed facilities, please see GAO, *National Airspace System: Improved Budget Process Could Help FAA Better Determine Future Operations and Maintenance Priorities,* GAO-13-693 (Washington, D.C.: Aug. 22, 2013).

through leases or other types of agreements under which the (non-federal) owner is responsible for maintenance. These include air traffic control towers and administrative facilities that serve a variety of functions.[8]

Table 1: Maintenance Responsibilities for FAA's Staffed Facilities, 2013

Facility Description	Responsible entity (number of facilities)			Total
	FAA	GSA	Other (including non-federal)	
En-route Traffic Control Facilities	23	-	-	**23**
Terminal facility sites, including Air Traffic Control Towers and Terminal Radar Approach Control (TRACON) facilities	402	-	137	**539[a]**
FAA Mke Monroney Aeronautical Center[b]	37	-	23	**60**
FAA William J. Hughes Technical Center	43	-	-	**43**
Administrative/Other	-	8	560[c]	**568**
Total	**505**	**8**	**720**	**1233**

Source: GAO analysis of FAA and GSA data.

Note: FAA maintains some facilities that are not federally owned. For example, under the terms of some lease agreements, FAA maintains terminal facilities that are owned by non-federal entities such as airport authorities.

[a] Some of the terminal facility sites contain more than one facility. According to FAA facility data, there are 543 facilities at these sites.

[b] In 2013, Aeronautical Center staff occupy 60 facilities that include facilities that are either federally owned or leased from the Oklahoma City Airport Trust, which has primary responsibility for their maintenance. The Aeronautical Center also has an additional 68 federally maintained and leased facilities that are considered unstaffed.

[c] This includes 33 facilities that GSA leases on behalf of FAA for FAA staff; the property owners are responsible for their maintenance.

---

[8] Examples of FAA's administrative offices include its Certificate Management Office (CMO), Flight Standards District Office (FSDO), and Manufacturing Inspection District Office (MIDO). FAA's CMO is responsible for the certification, surveillance, and inspection of major air carriers and Flight Safety International's part 142 Training Centers; its FSDO responsibilities include airmen certification (licensing) for pilots, mechanics, repairmen, dispatchers, and parachute riggers; and the responsibilities of its MIDOs include airworthiness certification and the oversight of Manufacturing Designees.

GAO-13-757 Facilities Condition

GSA's and FAA's internal organizational components responsible for facility maintenance collect information on the condition of their respective facility portfolios. This generally includes information on the Facility Condition Index (FCI)[9] and deferred maintenance[10]—two widely used benchmarks to determine the relative condition of public and private facilities. However, because of the variation in methods used to determine condition, the condition data for one type of facility may not be comparable to that for another type of facility. FAA also maintains an agency-wide Real Estate Management System (REMS) to collect information, including FCI data, on facilities in its inventory. FAA uses REMS for reporting required information to the Federal Real Property Profile (FRPP).[11]

Funding for facilities modernization, improvement, and replacement projects derives from FAA's Facilities and Equipment account.[12] The funding in this account is tied to the annually updated Capital Investment Plan, or CIP. This plan is to identify planned capital investments for the next 5 years consistent with the amount requested in FAA's annual budget submission.

FAA Employees' Safety and Health

Two agencies within Labor administer programs related to safety and health issues in federal facilities: OSHA, which oversees compliance with occupational safety and health standards, and the Office of Workers' Compensation Programs (OWCP), which oversees certain programs to compensate employees for wages lost as a result of employment-related

---

[9] As a formula, FCI is the value of the maintenance, repair, and replacement deficiencies of a facility divided by its current replacement value. The resulting fraction is then subtracted from 1 to express FCI as a percentage. Facilities can be grouped according to FCI values. ATO, for example, defines a facility with an FCI above 95 percent as in "good" condition, 90 to 95 percent to be in "fair" condition, and below 90 percent to be in "poor" condition.

[10] For its en-route and terminal facilities, FAA defines deferred maintenance as the cost of rebuilding or replacing components whose service life has exceeded their scheduled lifetime as of the forecast year. FAA does not include preventative maintenance and minor repairs in its deferred maintenance calculations.

[11] FRPP is the inventory system for the federal real property portfolio. FRPP, which is overseen by OMB, includes data elements that agencies are mandated to report annually, including performance measures on asset utilization, condition, mission dependency, and operating cost.

[12] Two budget accounts provide the principal source of funding for FAA facilities. The Facilities and Equipment account funds major modernization and improvement projects while the Operations account funds routine maintenance and repairs.

injuries or illnesses. OSHA sets and enforces workplace standards affecting FAA facilities. As part of its enforcement efforts, OSHA conducts programmed and unprogrammed inspections of worksites to ensure compliance with its safety and health standards.[13] Among other things, OWCP adjudicates federal employees' claims for compensation resulting from employment-related injuries and illnesses. FAA staff who sustain employment-related injuries and illnesses may file a workers' compensation claim with FAA for subsequent transmittal to OWCP.[14]

In addition, as required by law, FAA administers an environmental and occupational safety and health (EOSH) program that includes inspections aimed at preventing workplace injuries.[15] Under its EOSH program, FAA annually inspects each of its staffed facilities and maintains inspection results in a central database. Also, under its EOSH program, FAA established Occupational Safety, Health, and Environmental Compliance Committees (OSHECCOM) to provide a method for employees to use their knowledge of workplace operations to assist agency management in improving policies, conditions, and practices concerning safety and health matters in agency workplaces.

---

[13] OSHA's programmed inspections are scheduled investigations that target specific worksite hazards or high-hazard industries and worksites. OSHA's unprogrammed inspections are conducted in response to imminent danger, fatalities or catastrophes, complaints, referrals, and as follow-up and monitoring of prior inspections.

[14] For claims it approves, OWCP bases the benefits on an employee's wages at time of injury, the date the disability began or the date the disability recurred, his or her ability to work after the injury, and whether he or she has eligible dependents. OWCP charges agencies for the benefits provided to their injured employees. These agencies subsequently reimburse Labor's Employees' Compensation Fund from their next annual appropriation. Workers' compensation benefits paid to beneficiaries are adjusted for inflation and are not taxed or subject to age restrictions.

[15] See 29 U.S.C. § 668, 29 C.F.R. pt. 1960, and Exec. Order No. 12196, Occupational Safety and Health Programs for Federal Employees, 45 Fed. Reg. 12769 (Feb. 27, 1980).

FAA-Staffed Facilities Are Generally in "Good" to "Fair" Condition, but Opportunities Exist to Improve Assessment Methods and Condition Information

Most Federally Maintained Facilities Occupied by FAA Employees Are in "Good" to "Fair" Condition

According to data available for the federally maintained facilities occupied by FAA staff, facilities are generally in "good" to "fair" condition based on their FCIs.[16] This information results from the condition assessment processes and data sources used by each FAA organizational component that has facility maintenance responsibility as well as from GSA.[17] Specifically:

- ATO uses a technical-consulting firm to annually inspect a portion of en-route and terminal facilities. ATO's consultant annually produces "roll-up" reports that provide condition information for facilities that have been inspected during the current year as well as during the preceding 5-year period.[18] For terminal facilities not inspected over this time period, ATO's consultant estimates their condition by using

---

[16] See footnote 9.

[17] As discussed below, Technical Center managers use a process that assesses the conditions of a facility's components such as structural, electrical, and mechanical systems. This process does not yield an FCI for each facility but rather provides component-specific measures of condition.

[18] FAA's consultant inspects each en-route facility approximately once every 4 to 5 years, and "roll-up" reports for these facilities contain actual inspection results for each of the 23 facilities. For terminal facilities, roll-up reports contain actual inspection results from facilities inspected over the most recent 6-year period. FAA's most recent terminal facility roll-up report, for example, contains information from 128 facility sites inspected from January 2007 through December 2012.

the condition data from inspected facilities; these estimates are contained in the annual terminal facilities roll-up report.[19]

- Aeronautical Center managers use a technical-consulting firm to inspect their federally maintained facilities on a biennial basis. Aeronautical Center managers use condition data obtained through these inspections and update them between inspection cycles to reflect repairs or improvements made to those facilities.

- Technical Center managers used a technical contractor to inspect most of their federally maintained facilities in 2007 and 2008.[20] Technical Center managers use condition data derived from these inspections to determine what improvements are needed.

- GSA uses a standardized physical condition survey process administered by its on-site staff to biennially assess the condition of the facilities it maintains. GSA manages a database containing information derived from these surveys.

Because of variations in the methods used to determine condition, the condition data for one type of facility may not be comparable to that for another type of facility. Our analysis of condition by facility type is presented below.

En-route Air Traffic Control Centers and Terminal Facilities

According to ATO's most recent roll-up reports

- 23 en-route air traffic control centers are generally in "fair" condition having an aggregated FCI of 93.5 percent,[21] with deferred maintenance totaling approximately $98 million and replacement values totaling about $1.5 billion.

---

[19] FAA's consultant develops a statistical model based on data obtained from the inspected facilities to estimate the condition of facilities that have not been inspected. The model uses age to estimate the FCI and deferred maintenance of each facility not inspected.

[20] The inspection covered 34 of the 43 federally maintained staffed facilities at the Technical Center. Technical Center managers indicated that they intend to award a new contract by early fiscal year 2014 to inspect the 9 facilities not previously inspected in 2014.

[21] See footnote 9.

- 134 terminal facilities—the subset of terminal facilities that have been inspected—are at the transition from "good" to "fair" condition having an aggregated FCI of 94.9 percent, with deferred maintenance totaling about $82 million and replacement values totaling about $1.6 billion. [22]

- 409 terminal facilities—the subset of terminal facilities that have not been inspected—have estimated FCI and deferred maintenance values. Because FAA's estimates for these uninspected facilities have substantial errors, we do not present condition data for them. We discuss in greater detail below and in appendix II the imprecision of FAA's estimating method and alternatives for improving the accuracy of its estimates.

Based on our interviews with ATO and its technical consultant, we found the inspection and its related reporting process results are reliable indicators of the condition of inspected facilities based on generally accepted industry standards. However, as we explain below, limitations in ATO's process for estimating the condition of terminal facilities that have not been inspected may result in estimates that overstate or understate actual conditions. Moreover, based on our discussions with ATO and its technical consultant, we learned that condition data prior to 2010 were obtained using a different method than currently used. As a result, we determined that year-to-year comparison of condition data was appropriate only for data for inspected facilities from 2010 through 2012. Table 2 shows aggregate FCI and deferred maintenance values for en-route air traffic control centers and terminal facilities over this time period.

---

[22] If seismic codes and standards deficiencies are included, the aggregated FCI for the 128 sites is 87.9 percent, or "poor" condition.

GAO-13-757 Facilities Condition

Table 2: Aggregate FCI and Deferred Maintenance Values for En-route Air Traffic Control Centers and Inspected Terminal Facilities, 2010 through 2012 (Dollars in Millions)

Facility type	2010		2011		2012	
	FCI	Deferred maintenance	FCI	Deferred maintenance	FCI	Deferred maintenance
En-route centers	93.7%	$91	93.7%	$94	93.5%	$98
Inspected terminal facilities[a]	95.2	61.8	95.5	65.2	94.9	81.9

Source: National Roll-Up Reports for En-route Facilities and Final MARS Roll-Up Reports for ATCT-TRACON Sites, FAA.

Notes: Data for En-route Centers are based on the fiscal year while data for terminal facilities are based on the calendar year.

The aggregate FCI is the summed deferred maintenance values divided by the summed replacement values, subtracted from 1. The aggregate deferred maintenance values represent the summed deferred maintenance amounts across the relevant subset of facilities.

[a]The data shown are for only those terminal facilities that have been inspected and exclude deficiencies resulting from seismic, code, and standards assessments. For 2010, there were 114 inspected terminal facilities; for 2011, there were 121; and for 2012, there were 134.

Mike Monroney Aeronautical Center Facilities

According to fiscal year 2010 data, the aggregated FCI of 110 Aeronautical Center facilities is 95.2 percent, or "good" condition, based on deferred maintenance totaling about $6.5 million and replacement values totaling about $135 million.[23] Based on interviews with Aeronautical Center managers, we found the inspection method followed generally accepted industry standards and its related reporting process results and are reliable facility condition indicators.

William J. Hughes Technical Center Facilities

The Technical Center's inspection process does not yield facility-level condition data such as an FCI. Rather, the process assesses the conditions of the components—such as structural, electrical, and heating/cooling systems—that comprise each facility. Because available data for Technical Center facilities does not reflect facility-level conditions

---

[23] This includes both staffed and unstaffed facilities. According to Aeronautical Center officials, unstaffed facilities include guard sheds, shelters for NAS equipment, and other services such as Digital Remote Switching. Further, this deferred-maintenance estimate does not include costs for design services, demolition and restoration of architectural finishes, staging, moving services, and other expenses related to completion of the associated maintenance and repair work.

GAO-13-757 Facilities Condition

similar to what we reported for other facility types, we do not present them in this report.

GSA-Maintained FAA Facilities

According to GSA data, the 8 staffed facilities it maintains for FAA have FCIs ranging from 95 percent ("good" condition) to 46 percent ("poor" condition).[24] GSA-maintained facilities where FAA is the principal occupant are the Hawthorne Federal Building (46.0 percent FCI), Orville Wright Building (82.0 percent FCI), and Wilbur Wright Building (90.0 percent FCI).[25] We found the facilities condition data for the FAA facilities that GSA maintains to be reliable indicators of these facilities.[26] We also observed that GSA uses a different convention than FAA in categorizing facilities based on their FCI values. This results in GSA's having different FCI thresholds than FAA for determining if a facility is in "good," "fair," or "poor" condition.[27]

REMS Facility Condition Data Differ from Those Maintained by ATO and the Aeronautical Center

FAA collects information on all facilities in its portfolio (both federally owned and leased) and enters the data in REMS, FAA's repository for its entire real-property inventory. Information maintained in REMS includes the location, size, age, plant replacement value, operations and maintenance costs, repair needs, and FCI data for facilities. REMS is overseen by FAA's Aviation Logistics Organization (ALO), which provides guidance for users on updating REMS facilities data. FAA uses REMS for reporting required information to the FRPP.[28]

---

[24] These facilities include the Orville Wright Building (Washington, D.C.), Wilbur Wright Building (Washington, D.C.), Hawthorne Federal Building (Hawthorne, CA), Senator Paul Simon Federal Building (Carbondale, IL), Prince J. Kuhio Federal Building and U.S. Courthouse (Honolulu, HI), and the Anchorage Federal Building and U.S. Courthouse & Annex (Anchorage, AK). FAA may be the sole tenant or part of a multi-tenant occupancy of these facilities.

[25] FCI information may not reflect current conditions. For example, in January 2013, we visited the Hawthorne Federal Building, which is located in FAA's Western-Pacific Region, and saw that the roof had been replaced, which should result in a higher FCI for the facility when it is next assessed.

[26] Appendix I describes in further detail the steps taken to determine the reliability of the data.

[27] GSA views an FCI of 90 percent and above as "good" condition, between 70 and 90 percent as "fair" condition, and less than 70 percent as "poor" condition.

[28] See footnote 11.

We initially assessed REMS data to obtain information on the condition of the agency's facilities but found it was not reliable for this purpose. For example, 16.5 percent (141) of the records for non-leased facilities in the initial REMS file FAA provided us had missing FCIs or an FCI of zero.[29] We also found that the FCI data obtained from ATO and the Aeronautical Center did not consistently match FCI data in REMS. REMS uses an FCI that was modeled on DOD's facility-pricing index while ATO's and the Aeronautical Center's engineering consultants calculate FCIs from actual inspections.[30] FAA officials recognized that ATO's and the Aeronautical Center's FCI data were more robust and indicated that we should use their data in lieu of REMS in our assessment of facilities that are maintained by FAA.

Throughout the course of our review, we brought to ALO's attention deficiencies that we found with REMS, such as facilities with wrong addresses, incorrect use status, and erroneous lease costs. Furthermore, ALO independently recognized shortcomings with REMS and informed us that it has also been trying to correct errors with the data as well as address deficiencies we identified.[31] For example, Aeronautical Center officials told us that whenever they tried to update REMS with their FCI data, the updated condition data would revert back to the original REMS data after a certain period of time. FAA officials and the consulting firm that manages REMS told us that a "business rule" in the programming for REMS caused the condition data updates entered by Aeronautical Center staff to be overwritten, causing the accurate up-to-date data to be replaced by the old data. ALO recently agreed to change this "business rule" to prevent updated facility condition data from being overwritten. In addition, ALO has taken steps to correct the errors with address, use status, and lease data. For example, ALO recently found 13 cases of an air traffic control tower noted as "unstaffed" and updated the database to show their use as staffed facilities. ALO officials also plan to replace the different identifiers currently used in REMS for denoting an air traffic control tower with just one primary identifier. ALO officials agreed that

---

[29] While FAA is required to maintain information on leased properties in REMS, FCIs are not one of the required data elements for these facilities.

[30] According to FAA officials, the REMS model for estimating FCI incorporates the DOD *Facilities Pricing Guide* in part because FAA has comparable facilities to DOD, such as air traffic control towers.

[31] In response to our questions about REMS data, FAA sent us revised REMS data sets on at least three different occasions.

REMS data need to be better synchronized with other real property data in FAA's other organizational components. To be better stewards of FAA's real property, on June 24, 2013, FAA chartered a property accountability board—a cross-organizational entity that is to continue to undertake strategic, management, and operational initiatives to improve property management.

We are encouraged with the steps FAA is taking to address the REMS deficiencies we identified to ensure a strong data validation and correction process, but the extent to which other deficiencies exist is not clear as FAA has not comprehensively assessed the quality of REMS data and raises questions as to whether the database is a useful tool for managing FAA's facilities portfolio. Federal internal control standards state that agencies have relevant, reliable, and timely information for decision-making and external-reporting purposes.[32] This is enabled by sound and consistent data collection practices that ensure data are reasonably complete and accurate. OMB also has data quality guidelines for ensuring quality in information disseminated by federal agencies.[33] Furthermore, leading practices for using information to make capital-investment decisions call for a needs assessment that makes use of an accurate and up-to-date inventory of assets as well as current information on their condition.[34] Comprehensively assessing the quality of the REMS data, determining if the data are appropriate for their intended use, and implementing corrective actions, as needed, to ensure that data are sufficiently complete and accurate with data maintained among other FAA organizational components would provide FAA with better assurance that its source for facilities information agencywide is reliable for making informed decisions.

---

[32]GAO, *Standards for Internal Control in the Federal Government*, GAO/AIMD-00-21.3.1 (Washington, D.C.: November 1999).

[33] Office of Management and Budget, "Guidelines for Ensuring and Maximizing the Quality, Objectivity, Utility, and Integrity of Information Disseminated by Federal Agencies." 67 Fed. Reg. 8452 (Feb. 22, 2002). Those guidelines state that, among other things, agencies "shall adopt a basic standard of quality (including objectivity, utility, and integrity) as a performance goal and should take appropriate steps to incorporate information quality criteria into agency information dissemination practices."

[34] See footnote 6.

FAA's Method of Assessing the Condition of Uninspected Terminal Facilities Produces Error and Uncertainty

As indicated above, ATO uses a statistical method to estimate the condition of most terminal facilities; however, the limitations of this method produce estimates with substantial error and uncertainty. ATO has current inspection data for approximately one quarter of all terminal facilities (based on a 6-year rolling count of inspected facilities[35]) and estimates the condition of the remaining facilities that have not been inspected. ATO's consulting firm annually develops a statistical model based on data obtained from the inspected facilities to estimate the condition of facilities that have not been inspected. In particular, the model uses facility age to estimate the FCI and deferred maintenance of each facility not inspected. In 2012, for example, ATO's consultant developed a statistical model based on inspection results of 134 inspected facilities to estimate the FCI and deferred maintenance at 409 facilities not inspected. ATO's 2012 terminal facilities "roll-up" report presents condition information for these facilities.

The following example derived from this roll-up report illustrates the limitations of using facility age as the sole determinant in estimating FCI and deferred maintenance. In the 2012 roll-up report, eight air traffic control towers, each 17 years old, were identified as having the same FCI and deferred maintenance amount, about 96.5 percent and around $215,000 respectively, as estimated based on age (see fig. 1). However, given differences in their locations, sizes, number of flight operations managed, and physical components, actual conditions at each are likely different. For example, two of these towers are located at two of the busiest airports in the country, Chicago, IL, and Los Angeles, CA. These towers are larger and experience more wear than other towers as a result of comparatively greater use by controllers. During our visit to the Los Angeles tower, officials showed us the single elevator that services the tower's cab and described its maintenance issues.[36] These officials noted, at the time of our visit in January 2013, that this elevator had experienced 17 outages since May 2012 and would cost about $500,000 to repair.[37]

---

[35] See footnote 18.

[36] The cab is the elevated component of the air traffic control tower where controllers direct ground traffic, takeoffs, and landings.

[37] According to officials at the tower, the elevator will undergo repairs in September 2013, partially funded by resources diverted from a repair project at another facility.

Figure 1: Eight FAA Air Traffic Control Towers Reported to Have the Same FCI and Deferred Maintenance Amount

ATO's model predicts that these 8 air traffic control towers have exactly the same FCI (about 96.5 percent) and deferred maintenance (about $215,000) because they are all 17 years old, and age is the sole independent variable the model uses to predict FCI and deferred maintenance. However, given differences among tower locations, flight operations patterns, and facility structures, actual conditions at each tower are likely different.

Bangor International
(Bangor, Maine)

Total operations: 25,995
Tower cab area (square feet): 350
Tower height (in feet): 111

Bellingham International
(Bellingham, Washington)

Total operations: 16,914
Tower cab area (square feet): 365
Tower height (in feet): 58

Los Angeles International
(Los Angeles, California)

Total operations: 603,381
Tower cab area (square feet): 665
Tower height (in feet): 252

Montgomery Regional
(Montgomery, Alabama)

Total operations: 28,937
Tower cab area (square feet): 380
Tower height (in feet): 109

Chicago O'Hare International
(Chicago, Illinois)

Total operations: 874,561
Tower cab area (square feet): 1,100
Tower height (in feet): 230

Worcester Regional
(Worcester, Massachusetts)

Total operations: 3,556
Tower cab area (square feet): 350
Tower height (in feet): 100

San Diego International
(San Diego, California)

Total operations: 183,985
Tower cab area (square feet): 477
Tower height (in feet): 104

Tallahassee Regional
(Tallahassee, Florida)

Total operations: 40,533
Tower cab area (square feet): 440
Tower height (in feet): 93

Sources: FAA (photographs) and GAO analysis of FAA data.

To quantify the accuracy of the methods ATO's consultant used to estimate the FCIs and deferred maintenance of uninspected terminal facilities shown in the 2012 roll-up report, we compared FCI and deferred maintenance data derived from actual inspection of 134 facilities[38] to what their estimated FCI and deferred maintenance values would be using the statistical model. In reference to FAA's general categorization of facilities in "good", "fair", or "poor" condition based on their FCI values, we found that 41 percent of the inspected facilities would have been reclassified using estimated rather than actual FCI values. In particular, the statistical model classified 32 of the 134 facilities (24 percent) in a better condition category than actual inspection data showed, and it classified 23 of 134 facilities (17 percent) in a worse condition category than actual inspection data showed. For deferred maintenance, we found that, in 2012, 94 percent of facilities had estimated deferred maintenance values that differed by greater than 10 percent from actual values.

As another approach to testing the accuracy of ATO's statistical model for estimating FCI and deferred maintenance, and assessing alternatives for improving the model, we used data presented in the 2010 roll-up report as described below. Appendix II presents a more detailed description of our analysis.

- Accuracy of FCI estimates. To assess the accuracy of FCI estimates, we compared actual FCI results (based on inspections) to the model's predictions for the same facilities. The goal was to calculate the uncertainty of the predicted FCIs, as calculated from the ATO model. We found that ATO's estimates were not highly precise. The model estimated that if ATO measured actual FCIs for a new sample of facilities, the actual FCIs would vary by an average of plus or minus 3.4 percentage points in 95 percent of the new samples. That is a moderately large error, given that the middle 50 percent of actual FCIs ranged from 90.9 to 96.6 percentage points. In other words, the margin of error of the estimates was almost as large as the range of the actual FCIs.

- Accuracy of deferred maintenance estimates. To assess the accuracy of deferred maintenance estimates, we compared actual deferred maintenance results (based on inspections) to the model's predictions for the same facilities. Similar to our findings on FCI estimates, we found that ATO's estimates for deferred maintenance were not highly precise. On average, the model's estimates varied from the actual

---

[38] While there are 128 facility sites inspected, some of those sites have more than one facility or tower. Condition data were obtained at 134 facilities within these 128 sites.

deferred maintenance by $606,862. This is a moderately large error, given that the middle 50 percent of actual deferred maintenance values ranged from $231,420 to $663,944 in this time period.

Our analysis shows that although FCI and deferred maintenance are correlated with age, the strength of the relationship is not strong enough to produce highly precise estimates of FCI and deferred maintenance for facilities that are not inspected. As a result, the true condition of the uninspected facilities is less precise and certain than FAA's roll-up reports suggest. Based on our analysis of FAA's data, we determined that increasing the number of variables in FAA's estimation method could potentially improve its accuracy. For example, we found that incorporating facility replacement value[39] into the model for estimating deferred maintenance significantly reduced the error and uncertainty of the estimates. Table 3 illustrates the difference in accuracy between the ATO consultant's use of age as the only factor to predict deferred maintenance and our use of age and facility replacement value. On average, our model predicted deferred maintenance with 39 percent less error than ATO's current approach.

Table 3: Comparison of Results from FAA and GAO Models for Estimating Deferred Maintenance at Selected Terminal Facilities (Dollars in Thousands)

Facility	Facility age (years)	Facility replacement value	Deferred maintenance – actual[a]	Deferred maintenance – FAA estimate[b]	Deferred maintenance – GAO estimate[c]
Dallas - Ft Worth TRACON (Texas)	36	$42,112	$2,893	$524	$3,143
Greensboro Tower (North Carolina)	36	7,506	1,173	524	592
Teterboro Tower (New Jersey)	36	4.215	289	524	349
Woodring Tower (Oklahoma)	36	3,129	150	524	269

[39] Facility replacement value is the total expenditure required to replace a facility, inclusive of construction, design, and project management and administrative costs.

Facility	Facility age (years)	Facility replacement value	Deferred maintenance – actual[a]	Deferred maintenance – FAA estimate[b]	Deferred maintenance – GAO estimate[c]
Yakima Tower (Washington)	36	3,487	295	524	296

Source: GAO analysis

[a]Actual deferred maintenance as shown in FAA's 2010 terminal facility roll-up report.
[b]Estimate based on FAA consultant's model using facility age to predict deferred maintenance.
[c] Estimate based on GAO model using facility age and facility replacement value to predict deferred maintenance.

For its part, ATO's consultant has documented in the roll-up reports the limitations of its model to estimate FCI and deferred maintenance and has recommended improvements, such as using facility size as a variable in the model. As indicated by our analysis, increasing the number of variables in the method for estimating FCI and deferred maintenance could potentially improve the FCI's accuracy, because the method would include other factors that are correlated with condition, such as usage and weather conditions. In addition, assessing and reporting the prediction error associated with any statistical estimate, regardless of the estimation method used, is useful in quantifying the degree to which the estimate varies from actual conditions. Also, inspecting the condition of a probability sample of terminal facilities, either as a supplement or alternative to FAA's current approach, may help ensure that FCI estimates accurately represent the population, particularly for reporting average and total condition across facilities. Having accurate and reliable facility condition data allows management to have a clear picture of repair needs that may affect future budget requests.[40]

---

[40] GAO, *Federal Buildings Fund: Improved Transparency and Long-term Plan Needed to Clarify Capital Funding Priorities*, GAO-12-646 (Washington, D.C.: July 12, 2012).

GAO-13-757 Facilities Condition

While the Number of Injuries and Illnesses Resulting in FAA's Workers' Compensation Claims Has Steadily Decreased from 2007 Through 2011, FAA Has Not Always Met Its Goals for Processing Claims

The Most Common Types of Injuries and Illnesses Claimed Include Orthopedic and Mental, Emotional, or Nervous Conditions

Workers' compensation claims filed by FAA employees and accepted by OWCP from 2007 through 2012[41] indicate that the five most common types of injuries and illnesses sustained by FAA employees ranged from mental, emotional, or nervous conditions to different types of orthopedic injuries (see table 4). According to FAA officials, orthopedic injuries represent the most frequent types of injuries filed by FAA employees and accepted by OWCP. These claims cite various causes of reported injuries and illnesses including falls, handling tools and materials, fume inhalation, and vehicle accidents. Workers' compensation claims data cannot be linked to facility conditions because of the variability of factors contributing to reported injuries and illnesses.

---

[41] OWCP data for 2012 are from January to September.

Table 4: Top Five Types of Injuries or Illnesses Claims Filed by FAA Employees and Accepted by OWCP, 2007 to 2012

Nature of injury	Number of Claims
Mental, emotional, or nervous condition	928
Back sprain/strain or back pain[a]	826
Sprain/strain of ligament, muscle, tendon (not back)[a]	700
Pain, swelling, redness, stiffness (not in joint)[a]	615
Joint pain/swelling/stiffness/redness[a]	472

Source: GAO analysis of Labor data.

Note: Data are based on the date of injury indicated on certified workers' compensation claims filed by FAA employees and accepted by OWCP. Data for 2012 are from January through September.

[a] FAA considers these injuries to be orthopedic injuries.

The Number of Workers' Compensation Claims Filed by FAA Employees and Accepted by OWCP Decreased from 2007 through 2011

The number of workers' compensation claims filed by FAA employees and accepted by OWCP has steadily decreased since 2007.[42] According to OWCP data, in 2011, 907 injuries resulted in workers' compensation claims filed by FAA employees that were accepted by OWCP—a decrease of 32 percent since 2007 (see fig. 2).[43] Over the same time period, the number of permanent FAA employees increased from 44,423 in 2007 to 47,242 in 2011. The ratio of the number of FAA employees to the number of workers' compensation claims filed by an FAA employee and accepted by OWCP has increased from 33:1 in 2007 to 52:1 in 2011 (see table 5).

[42] The Federal Employees' Compensation Act provides that a claim for compensation must be filed within 3 years of the date of injury. For a traumatic injury, the statutory time limitation begins to run from the date of injury. For a latent condition, it begins to run when an injured employee with a compensable disability becomes aware, or reasonably should have been aware, of a possible relationship between the medical condition and the employment.

[43] For this report, we are using the date of injury to track the number of new workers' compensation claims filed by FAA employees and accepted by OWCP each year. These figures do not include workers' compensation claims that were rejected by OWCP or injuries for which an employee did not file a claim.

Figure 2: Number of Workers' Compensation Claims of FAA Employees Accepted by OWCP, 2007 to 2012

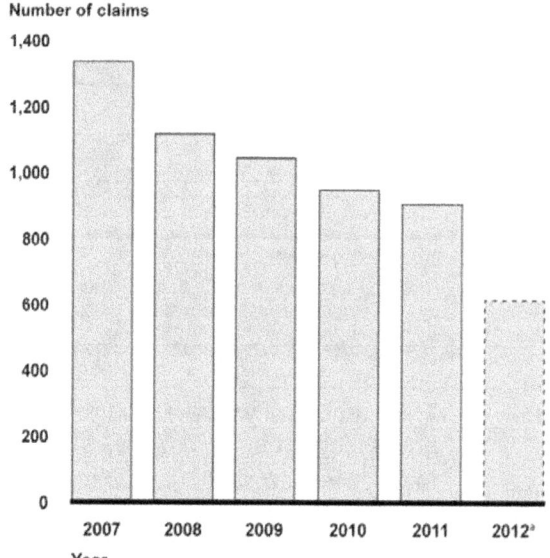

Number of claims

Year

Source: GAO analysis of Labor data.

Note: Data are based on the date of injury indicated on workers' compensation claims filed by FAA employees and accepted by OWCP.

[a] Data for 2012 are from January through September.

Table 5: Ratio of FAA Employees to Number of Claims Filed by FAA Employees and Accepted by OWCP, 2007 through 2011

	2007	2008	2009	2010	2011
Claims	1,336	1,118	1,045	949	907
Number of FAA employees	44,423	45,272	47,020	47,456	47,242
Employees per claim	33 :1	40 :1	45 :1	50 :1	52 :1

Source: GAO analysis of FAA and DOL OWCP data.

FAA's total annual workers' compensation claim payments remained relatively constant during this period, ranging from $87 million to $91 million (see table 6). According to FAA, the annual payments have remained constant due to the large number of claims it must pay out that were accepted from previous years. For example, in fiscal year 2012, FAA paid 2,885 workers' compensation claims at a total cost of $95 million. Of those claims, 766 were accepted from 1961 to 1983 and accounted for $46.7 million of the 2012 costs. An FAA official attributed the constant annual costs to the rising costs of medical care and the annual cost of living adjustment to the level of compensation being provided to FAA claimants.

Table 6: FAA's Total Annual Workers' Compensation Claims Payments, 2007 through 2012

	2007	2008	2009	2010	2011	2012
Annual Payments (millions of dollars)	$87.0	$90.9	$92.5	$91.0	$90.6	$94.9

Source: FAA data.

FAA Uses Various Measures to Track the Performance of Its Workers' Compensation Program

FAA tracks its performance in processing employees' workers' compensation claims on an annual basis. According to FAA, it is required to process an employee's workers' compensation claim (form CA-1 or CA-2) internally and send it to Labor's OWCP for evaluation within 10 business days or 14 calendar days. FAA typically sets an annual performance target relative to this requirement. From 2007 through 2012, FAA has both exceeded and missed the target twice. FAA did not set a target for 2 of the 6 years. See table 7 for the annual targets and year end performance.

Table 7: FAA CA-1 and CA-2 Filing Timeliness: Percentage within 14 Days, Fiscal Year 2007 through 2012

	2007	2008	2009	2010	2011	2012
Target	N/A	65.3	68.6	N/A	86.9	89.5
Year-end performance	77.1	83.0	84.4	85.0	85.0	87.3

Source: Labor data.

FAA also measures the performance of its workers' compensation program by comparing changes in the percentage of its workers' compensation costs against similar changes government-wide. From fiscal year 2007 to 2012, FAA's annual workers' compensation costs increased 9 percent ($87.0 million to $94.9 million) while the government-wide average increased 21 percent ($2.49 billion to $3.01 billion).

Each year, FAA also estimates the amount of compensation payments and continuation of pay avoided when FAA either challenges a claim of questionable veracity and it is subsequently denied by OWCP, or an employee returns to duty following a disabling work injury as a result of FAA case management actions. From 2007 to 2012, FAA's annual compensation payments and continuation of pay avoided estimates for workers' compensation payments ranged from $8 million to $26 million.

FAA Has Taken Steps to Identify and Abate Workplace Hazards

FAA's EOSH Program Includes Steps to Identify and Manage the Mitigation of Hazards

FAA has mechanisms to identify safety deficiencies at FAA facilities. For example, FAA annually conducts a safety and health inspection, as required by regulation,[44] at each of its staffed facilities[45] under its Environmental and Occupational Safety and Health (EOSH) program.[46] The goals of FAA's EOSH program are to (1) ensure a safe working environment, (2) establish a uniform, national workplace inspections process to identify hazards with the potential to cause injury, illness, or death, and (3) monitor and evaluate FAA's compliance with workplace inspection and hazard abatement requirements, measured against applicable federal, state, and local regulations. According to FAA, trained FAA employees or contractors perform the annual EOSH inspections. Before inspecting a facility, inspectors must review the injury/illness records, previous inspection reports, open findings, reports of unsafe and unhealthful working conditions, and employee complaints. After inspecting a facility, according to FAA, inspectors brief the facility's managers and then enter the results in FAA's Workplace Inspection Tool (WIT), which is a central database that management uses to track and ensure that identified safety and health hazards are mitigated.

As of March 15, 2013, FAA was tracking 123,368 separate hazards in WIT, with over 96 percent of those hazards abated and 4 percent open since WIT was implemented in October 2007. FAA officials stated that

---

[44] OSHA regulations require that all areas and operations of each workplace, including office operations, be inspected at least annually. 29 C.F.R. § 1960.25(c).

[45] FAA defines a "facility" as a physical location where agency work or operations are routinely performed and include offices, buildings, structures, work areas, equipment, and outside grounds associated with the facility.

[46] According to FAA, its occupational safety and health inspection program includes environmental aspects.

many of the open hazards are infrastructure-based improvements that will require significant funding to abate. For example, FAA reported that a $2 million infrastructure-based improvement is needed to abate extensive water intrusion and mold, which has caused the closure of three levels of the air traffic control tower at the San Juan, Puerto Rico, airport. The WIT was initially used by ATO but was recently expanded to the rest of FAA because of its effectiveness, according to FAA.

FAA Contracted for an Evaluation of EOSH Programs

To better understand and improve its EOSH program, FAA commissioned a consultant's study, issued in December 2012, to evaluate the EOSH programs across the agency. The report concluded that ATO has established the most comprehensive program within the FAA. However, the report also noted that 8 out of 11 organizational components evaluated were either unaware of their responsibilities or had undertaken little or no action to implement a complaint program. According to FAA officials, ATO's EOSH program will absorb the EOSH programs of the other organizational components to mitigate the issues described in the report and ensure a uniform approach to workplace safety.

FAA Established Safety Committees

In June 2008, FAA established an Occupational Safety, Health, and Environmental Compliance Committee (OSHECCOM) at the National, Region, Center, and field levels.[47] The committees were created to provide a method for employees to use their knowledge of workplace operations to assist agency management in improving polices, conditions, and practices. The role of OSHECCOM is to assist FAA's organizational components in maintaining an open channel of communication between employees and management concerning safety and health matters in the workplace.[48]

---

[47] In March 1996, FAA originally established an OSHECCOM and reemphasized that effort in June 2008 with a revised charter.

[48] Specifically, the OSHECCOM works to (1) establish a culture within FAA that facilitates an effective occupational safety, health, and environmental program; (2) improve intra-agency cooperation by establishing communication across the organizational components and promote a comprehensive occupational safety, health, and environmental program that can be implemented at all operational levels; (3) provide an open line of communication between management and nonmanagement employees regarding EOSH related matters; (4) monitor, assist, and support FAA's EOSH program; and (5) create a forum to address and discuss EOSH issues without fear of reprisal.

According to FAA, the national OSHECCOM has improved the EOSH program. For example, the national OSHECCOM implemented a cardiopulmonary resuscitation and automated external defibrillator program that trained thousands of FAA employees to render emergency medical care to individuals in FAA facilities. According to FAA officials, FAA employees used the training at an airline training facility in Texas to save the life of a pilot who was in cardiac arrest. FAA's employee union organizations stated that the OSHECCOMs, on the national level, have improved the level of communication between FAA and employees and that they expect it to continue to improve as the EOSH programs from the rest of FAA are moved under ATO's EOSH program. In addition, according to union officials we met with at the Aeronautical Center, the center's OSHECCOM was able to identify and mitigate serious pedestrian safety issues on the center's campus.

FAA Has Established Other Mechanisms to Report Safety Hazards at FAA Facilities

FAA employees may also report any hazards they identify to FAA managers at their facility or, as applicable, to their union representative or OSHA. According to FAA, facility managers then work to abate the hazard. In addition, FAA has agreements with employee union organizations to report safety concerns. Specifically, the Air Traffic Safety Action Program is an agreement between FAA and the National Air Traffic Controllers Association and the National Association of Government Employees that is designed to foster a voluntary, cooperative, nonpunitive environment for FAA air traffic employees to openly report safety concerns. Similarly, the Technical Operations Safety Action Program (T-SAP) is an agreement between FAA and the Professional Aviation Safety Specialists (PASS) that allows technicians represented by PASS and other non-bargaining unit Technical Operations employees the opportunity to report potential safety hazards voluntarily and confidentially. T-SAP is still a demonstration program, only available to employees in the Central Service Area, but FAA plans to expand this program.

OSHA Inspections Provide Another Mechanism to Promote Workplace Safety

OSHA conducted inspections at 153 FAA facilities from 2007 to 2012. Of these inspections, 57 were unprogrammed, including those originating from employee complaints such as unsafe egress. The 96 other inspections were programmed inspections that targeted specific worksite hazards or high-hazard worksites. OSHA began one such targeted inspection program to focus on concerns related to egress and fire safety at federally owned air traffic control towers operated by FAA. Under OSHA's Airport Traffic Control Tower Monitoring Inspection Program (AIRTRAF), which was conducted from 2008 to 2010, OSHA found deficiencies at 70 of the 75 air traffic control towers it inspected.[49] Specifically, 279 violations were cited at the 70 towers. The most frequently cited violations at the towers were for the lack of smoke/fire stops throughout the towers, missing exit signage in emergency egress routes, storage of combustible materials, and failure to conduct stair pressurization-system testing. According to OSHA, as of February 2013, FAA has corrected these deficiencies, and all 75 towers now comply with the applicable egress and fire safety standards. Of the remaining towers, according to FAA, 77 are currently not compliant with OSHA standards for egress and fire safety, with an estimated cost of $57.5 million to repair them. According to FAA officials, it will take 4 years to upgrade the remaining towers to meet egress and fire safety standards.

FAA Has Taken Steps to Strengthen Its Capital-Planning Process and Investment-Decision Practices That Are Generally Consistent with Leading Practices

FAA has taken steps to strengthen its capital-planning process to ensure its facilities are in good condition. We identified leading practices for using information to make capital-investment decisions primarily from GAO's Executive Guide and OMB's Capital Programming Guide (see table 8).[50] We also drew from leading capital investment practices identified by the National Research Council. We compared FAA's actions related to capital-planning and investment-decision making—focusing on operations facilities since they are the principal type of facility FAA maintains—to the criteria established in these guides.

---

[49] Because the unique design of air traffic control towers poses challenges to meeting standard OSHA egress and fire safety requirements, FAA developed an alternate standard specific to these facilities. Under its AIRTRAF inspection program, OSHA assessed air traffic control towers against this alternate standard.

[50] See footnote 6.

Table 8: Leading Capital-Planning Practices for Using Information to Make Capital-Investment Decisions

Leading practices	Description
Needs assessment	A comprehensive needs assessment identifies the resources needed to fulfill both immediate requirements and anticipated future needs based on the results-oriented goals and objectives that flow from the organization's mission. A comprehensive assessment of needs considers the capability of existing resources and makes use of an accurate and up-to-date inventory of capital assets and facilities, as well as current information on asset condition. Using this information, an organization can make decisions about where to invest in facilities.
Review and approval of framework with established criteria for selecting capital investments	Agencies should establish a formal process for senior management to review and approve proposed capital assets. The cost of a proposed asset, the level of risk involved in acquiring the asset, and its importance to achieving the agency mission should be considered when defining criteria for executive review. Leading organizations have processes that determine the level of review and analysis based on the size, complexity, and cost of a proposed investment or its organization wide impact. As a part of this framework, proposed capital investments should be compared to one another to create a portfolio of major assets ranked in priority order.
Project prioritization	Leading organizations have processes in which proposed capital investments should be compared to one another to create a portfolio of major assets ranked in priority order.
Strategic linkage	Capital planning is an integral part of an agency's strategic-planning process. It provides a long-range plan for the capital asset portfolio in order to meet the goals and objectives in the agency's strategic and annual performance plans. Agency strategic and annual performance plans should identify capital assets and define how they will help the agency achieve its goals and objectives. Leading organizations also view strategic planning as the vehicle that guides decision making for all spending.
Long-term capital plan	The long-term capital plan should be the final and principal product resulting from the agency's capital-planning process. The capital plan should cover 5 years or more and should reflect decision makers' priorities for the future. Leading organizations update long-term capital plans either annually or biennially. Agencies are encouraged to include certain elements in their capital plans, including a statement of the agency mission, strategic goals and objectives; a description of the agency's planning process; baseline assessments and identification of performance gaps; and a risk management plan.

Source: GAO and OMB.

Needs Assessment

Leading practices suggest that to establish a baseline of condition and needs, organizations should maintain systems that track the use and performance of existing assets. FAA's organizational components with responsibilities for managing facilities—ATO, the Aeronautical Center, and the Technical Center—have utilized technical consultants to inspect and determine the relative condition of building structures and systems. The inspections have resulted in the development of maintenance and repair requirements to correct identified deficiencies as documented in summary reports. For example, ATO's terminal and en-route and Aeronautical Center's facility inspection reports show maintenance and repair requirements for major components at each facility.[51] Similarly, the Technical Center's master plan contains component-specific information for facilities that indicate operability or need for replacement.

Leading practices also indicate that a comprehensive assessment of needs uses an accurate and up-to-date inventory of facilities as well as current information on their condition. While FAA's consultants' inspections provide current information on the condition of inspected facilities, the information on the condition of facilities that have not been inspected may be inaccurate. As previously discussed, ATO estimates the condition of most of the terminal facilities, and the method used to make the estimates produces results that may inaccurately reflect actual conditions and associated maintenance and repair needs. As a result, FAA cannot accurately determine any performance gap between current and needed conditions at its terminal facilities and is at risk of making suboptimal decisions about where to invest in maintenance and repairs.

Review and Approval of Framework with Established Criteria for Selecting Capital Investments

Leading practices call for a comprehensive decision-making framework to review, rank, and select from among competing project proposals. Such a framework should include the appropriate levels of management review, and selections should be based on established criteria. In January 2012, FAA created a Facilities Group Manager position within ATO to coordinate management of all its operations facilities, both staffed and unstaffed. Prior to this organizational change, managers of the different facility types—terminal facilities, en-route centers, and unstaffed facilities—acted independently in identifying requirements and prioritizing facility modernization and replacement projects. According to the Facilities Group Manager, under this previous organizational structure program managers of the different facility types competed with each other for funding and did not ensure common practices in planning and implementing modernization and replacement projects. As a result, managers likely applied different criteria in determining requirements and prioritizing projects so that investment decisions might not have addressed the most important needs of the operations facilities (ATO) portfolio. Going forward, the Facilities Group Manager's goal is to ensure

---

[51] Major building components include air handling units and ductwork, electrical distribution panels, lighting fixtures, lightning protection systems, uninterruptible power systems, and emergency generators, among others.

the use of common criteria to prioritize projects across facility types and make investment decisions that best align with mission needs.

Project Prioritization

FAA organizational components responsible for managing facilities incorporate elements of leading practices in their approaches to prioritizing capital-investment projects. Leading capital-planning practices suggest that project prioritization processes use weighted criteria and consider long-term capital plans and project risk. FAA organizational components with facility management responsibility currently use weighted criteria that reflect risk considerations as illustrated by the following descriptions of their prioritization processes.

- En-route centers: ATO's process for prioritizing projects at its en-route centers weighs proposals (in decreasing order of importance) on their (1) direct operational requirement, (2) safety impact, (3) indirect operational requirement, and (4) FCI. ATO considers risk and places the most significant weight on projects to correct deficiencies that present direct risk to the safety of the National Airspace System (NAS).

- Terminal facilities: In prioritizing projects for its terminal facilities, ATO categorizes requirements in eight categories (in decreasing order of importance): (1) waterproofing; (2) heating, ventilation, and air conditioning; (3) electrical; (4) elevators; (5) plumbing; (6) operations areas special needs; (7) exterior components; and (8) interior finishes. ATO then assigns a priority rating to projects giving highest priority to items that are degrading, where mitigation is difficult, and where adverse impacts regularly occur. Lower priority is assigned in cases where previously planned repairs and improvements are anticipated to address identified needs.

- Technical Center: Technical Center bases its prioritization on the condition codes and importance factors assigned to individual components of its facilities. According to the Technical Center, each of the projects it has identified to date has been to repair or replace components that were in the poorest condition and of the greatest importance.

- Aeronautical Center: The Aeronautical Center determines its project prioritization list based on three factors: (1) FCI of the facility, (2) mission criticality, and (3) a facility designation factor. The Aeronautical Center first identifies facilities with an FCI below 95 percent and subsequently eliminates facilities that are planned for demolition or whose FCI is low based on deferred maintenance for non-critical building components. The remaining facilities are then ranked using the following two factors, FAA mission criticality[52] and FAA facility designation.[53] Once a facility receives an overall ranking, the Center does a more in-depth study on the facility's actual condition and a business case analysis to determine detailed requirements.

In reference to operations facilities, as indicated previously, ATO's Facilities Group Manager is taking steps to develop a standard process for prioritizing projects across all facility types (en-route centers, terminal facilities, and unstaffed facilities). This single process is to replace the separate prioritization processes for en-route centers and terminal facilities described above. The new process considers operations, risk, employee safety, mission-critical needs, and environmental requirements as prioritization criteria. According to FAA officials, the new project prioritization process will be fully implemented by the fiscal year 2015 budget cycle.

Strategic Linkage and Long-term Capital Plan

Leading practices stress the importance of linking capital asset investments to an organization's overall mission and long-term strategic goals and the development of a long-term capital investment plan to guide the implementation of those organizational goals and objectives and to help decision makers establish priorities over time. FAA has capital asset investment-planning efforts under way related to the consolidation of operations facilities and the transition to NextGen, key strategic initiatives of the agency. These planning efforts include:

- En-route center and TRACON consolidation: In November 2011, FAA approved an initial plan to consolidate en-route centers and TRACONs into six large, integrated facilities over the next two decades (through 2034). This long-term plan realigns and

---

[52] Mission critical assets are those that house high-cost, mission critical equipment and technological systems, or assets that support the continuity of operations at the Aeronautical Center.

[53] FAA facility designation ranking is based on human occupancy levels and building size. The ranking with the highest score is a facility with over 151 employees and over 80,000 square feet of space. The next ranking is a facility with between 11 and 150 employees and 2,500 to 80,000 square feet of space. The lowest ranking is for a facility with 10 or fewer employees and less than 2,500 square feet of space.

consolidates facilities based on operations, airspace responsibility, and geographic location. As we have previously concluded, reconfiguring facilities that handle air traffic control will be required to fully realize NextGen's capabilities, reduce operating costs in the long term, and address sustainability issues with FAA's current facility footprint.[54] However, according to FAA officials, the implementation of this plan has been delayed due to significant funding reductions.

- Terminal facility consolidation: FAA has been developing a national facilities consolidation report in response to the FAA Modernization and Reform Act of 2012. The act requires FAA to make recommendations for realigning and consolidating FAA services and facilities and provide justification, projected costs and savings, and proposed timing for implementing each recommendation.[55] FAA officials told us that the agency chartered a collaborative workgroup with labor unions to develop a process to address the act's requirements. Their efforts will focus on TRACON realignments and consolidation. In July 2013, FAA officials noted that they had developed a process for identifying potential facilities for consolidation and realignment and were evaluating realignment options as required by the act, but had not yet identified which facilities would be consolidated or realigned or a time frame for developing such a list.[56]

- En-route and Terminal facility "Get Well" plan: ATO's Facilities Group Manager is leading development of a 10-year plan that, among other things, establishes an approach to reduce the maintenance backlog at its existing facilities. According to data provided by the Facilities Group Manager in May 2013, ATO's current overall deferred maintenance backlog for staffed operations facilities is $258.8

---

[54] GAO, *Department of Transportation: Key Issues and Management Challenges, 2013,* GAO-13-402T (Washington, D.C.: Mar. 14, 2013).

[55] FAA Modernization and Reform Act of 2012, Pub. L. No. 112-95, § 804, 126 Stat.11,120 (Feb. 14, 2012).

[56] Additionally, FAA's contract with the air traffic controllers' union requires that FAA notify the union as soon as possible but not less than one year in advance of the closure of a facility, facility consolidation, or inter-facility reorganization requiring reassignment of employees. This provision, along with the status of FAA's realignment and consolidation efforts, suggests that it will be no less than 2 years before realignments and consolidations occur.

million.[57] The plan will be based on meeting a target FCI of 95 percent for all facilities and establish compliance with safety requirements as a primary focus. ATO expects to complete this plan by September 2013.

These planning efforts are important to FAA's ability to balance facility sustainment needs with NextGen requirements to ensure proper prioritization of projects. FAA's Capital Investment Plan (CIP) provides insight into the agency's long-term strategies for meeting these requirements. Leading practices emphasize the importance of developing a long-term capital investment plan to guide the implementation of organizational goals and objectives and to help decision makers establish priorities over time. Among the information provided in FAA's CIP is projected funding for budget line items (BLI) for facility improvements and replacement as informed by the outcomes of the project prioritization processes discussed above. For example, table 9 illustrates BLIs specific to funding en-route-center and terminal-facility improvement and replacement projects. This shows that FAA's fiscal year 2014 through 2017 forecasts—with the exception of the terminal replacement budget line—are generally greater than actual past funding levels and significantly greater than levels in fiscal year 2013. ATO officials attributed increases in these budget lines in part to the better understanding of costs to upkeep facilities gained from its facility condition assessments. In reference to en-route centers, ATO officials noted another reason for expected increases in future budgets is a result of the aging of facilities that last received an influx of funds for modernization projects in the early 1990s. Overall, ATO officials expect these forecast funding levels to result in a decrease in deferred maintenance and help them achieve their 95 percent FCI target for facilities.

---

[57] This amount comprises about 6 percent of FAA's total deferred maintenance backlog for all staffed and unstaffed facilities. According to FAA officials, the backlog increases to $4.6 billion when factoring in the deferred maintenance for power systems, fuel storage tanks, and power cables as well as backlogs associated with environmental compliance and cleanup requirements. FAA expects this overall backlog is expected to grow to $7.5 billion in 2024. However, as we note earlier in this report, we have concerns regarding how FAA estimates the condition and deferred maintenance of those facilities that have not been inspected.

Table 9: FAA's Actual and Projected Capital Improvement Budget Line Items, Fiscal Years 2008 through 2017 (Dollars in Millions)

Budget line item	Actual						Projected			
	2008	2009	2010	2011	2012	2013	2014	2015	2016	2017
En-route center improvements	50.0	55.5	48.7	35.4	39	38.5	50.0	61.1	58.0	60.0
Terminal facility replacement	162.6	136.5	171.2	71.6	51.6	64.9	72.0	96.0	100.0	110.0
Terminal facility improvements	40.4	36.3	37.3	43.8	49.3	18.7	50.0	50.2	50.0	50.0

Source: FAA CIP data for fiscal years 2008 through 2017.

However, budget uncertainty may limit ATO's ability to fund facilities projects as forecasted as well as limit efforts to implement facility consolidation and NextGen transition plans. The Balanced Budget and Emergency Deficit Control Act of 1985, as amended,[58] places limits on discretionary spending through 2021. ATO officials indicated that in preparing the update to the CIP, they recognize that future funding levels may be less than forecast in the current plan. As a result, they are developing a two-tier system to prioritize projects. For example, instead of maintaining all facilities at a 95 percent FCI, they would focus on maintaining only facilities at the 56 busiest airports at this level and facilities at all other airports at a 90 percent FCI.

Conclusions

FAA staff occupy an array of facility types including air traffic control towers, administrative offices, and research laboratories in executing the agency's mission to safely operate the NAS. The work environment defined by the condition of these facilities affects the safety and health of FAA employees. Inspecting facilities to gain information on their condition is important to FAA's ability to identify repair and modernization requirements and direct resources to address them. However, FAA's estimates of the condition of most terminal facilities—which represent a large segment of all FAA facilities—are inaccurate and lead to uncertainty in defining maintenance and repair needs. In addition, inaccuracies in

---

[58] Pub. L. No. 99-177, title II, §§ 251–251A, 99 Stat. 1037 (Dec. 12, 1985), as amended.

FAA's agency-wide REMS data source and inconsistent data collection practices contribute to causing uncertainty about the composition and condition of its facility portfolio. Accurate and reliable information on facility condition is important not only to providing a safe and healthy working environment but also to prioritizing long-term needs for providing a physical infrastructure that enables FAA to effectively meet its mission while working to consolidate facilities and transition to NextGen. Having accurate and reliable information on facility conditions and associated maintenance and repair needs will help FAA optimize use of its resources, which are likely to be constrained in future years as a result of budget controls, and align its strategic and capital plans to reflect these constraints.

Recommendations

To ensure that FAA has accurate and reliable information on the condition of its facilities and allow for more informed decision making on their maintenance and repairs and associated capital-planning efforts, we recommend that the Secretary of Transportation direct the FAA Administrator to take the following two actions:

- Improve the precision of the estimation methods used by ATO to determine conditions at terminal facilities that have not been inspected and assess and report the error associated with estimates of the terminal facilities' condition and deferred maintenance.

- Develop and implement a plan to comprehensively assess and improve REMS, consistent with sound data collection practices, to ensure that the data are sufficiently complete, accurate, and synchronized with other real property data maintained by FAA organizational components.

Agency Comments

We provided the Departments of Labor and Transportation and the General Services Administration with a draft of this report for review and comment. The Department of Transportation provided technical comments, which we incorporated as appropriate. Neither the Department of Labor nor the General Services Administration had comments on the draft report.

We are sending copies of this report to relevant congressional committees, the Secretary of Transportation, and other interested parties. In addition, this report will also be available at no charge on GAO's website at http://www.gao.gov.

If you or your staff have any questions about this report, please contact me at (202) 512-2834 or dillinghamg@gao.gov. Contact points for our Offices of Congressional Relations and Public Affairs may be found on the last page of this report. GAO staff who made key contributions to this report are listed in appendix III.

Gerald L. Dillingham, Ph.D.
Director, Physical Infrastructure

Appendix I: Objectives, Scope, and Methodology

Section 610 of the Federal Aviation Administration (FAA) Modernization and Reform Act of 2012 mandated GAO to study the condition of FAA-staffed facilities.[1] In response to this mandate, we addressed the following objectives:

1. What is known about the conditions of FAA-staffed facilities and to what extent are the assessment methods and resulting data reliable?

2. What have been the workplace injuries and illnesses reported by FAA employees in workers' compensation claims, and to what extent has FAA met its targets for processing claims?

3. To what extent has FAA responded to safety deficiencies identified through its inspections and those conducted by the Occupational Safety and Health Administration (OSHA)?

4. To what extent are actions FAA has taken to ensure that its facilities are in good condition, if any, consistent with leading practices for capital-investment decisions?

To determine what is known about the conditions of FAA-staffed facilities and the extent to which the methods used to make those determinations and the resulting data are reliable, we focused on staffed facilities that FAA or the General Services Administration (GSA) maintains.[2] We collected facility condition data from 2010 through 2012, including Facility Condition Indices (FCI) and deferred maintenance values for facilities, and compared the methods used by FAA and GSA in inspecting their facilities with generally accepted industry standards. Within FAA, we found two sources for facility condition data: the agency-wide Real Estate Management System (REMS) data and data from other FAA organizational components responsible for maintaining facilities. Early on, we found problems with REMS data and after discussions with REMS administrators and programmatic officials, we decided to use facility condition data from the FAA organizational components that are responsible for the facilities. Thus, we obtained facility data for en-route and terminal facilities from the Air Traffic Organization. We also obtained

---

[1] FAA Modernization and Reform Act of 2012, Pub. L. No. 112-95, § 610, 126 Stat. 11, 117 (Feb. 14, 2012).

[2] To differentiate responsibility for maintaining facilities, we use the phrase "FAA-maintained" or "GSA-maintained."

data from the Mike Monroney Aeronautical Center (Aeronautical Center) and the William J. Hughes Technical Center (Technical Center) for their facilities. For FAA's administrative facilities, we obtained condition data from the General Services Administration (GSA). The data we obtained represent different time frames (i.e., calendar year versus fiscal year). However, we used them because they were the only reliable data available. Further, the different sources of facility condition are based on differing methods. Therefore, in our analysis, we cannot compare the facility condition of one type of facility to other facility types. While we obtained the number of facilities leased by FAA and GSA, we did not obtain data on their condition because they did not exist or we determined that they were not reliable.

To assess the reliability of the FAA and GSA data we reviewed existing documentation about the data and interviewed agency officials and technical-consulting firm officials knowledgeable about the data. We performed electronic testing of the FAA data for obvious errors in accuracy and completeness. We found the data for FAA's en-route facilities, inspected terminal facilities, Aeronautical Center facilities, and GSA-maintained FAA facilities to be sufficiently reliable for describing facility condition. FAA's Technical Center's inspection process does not yield facility-level condition data, such as FCI. Rather, the process assesses the conditions of the components—such as structural, electrical, and heating/cooling systems—that comprise each facility. Because available data for Technical Center facilities does not reflect facility-level conditions similar to what we reported for other facility types, we do not present them in this report.

We did not find the condition data for FAA's uninspected terminal facilities to be reliable and conducted further analysis to articulate our concerns with the reliability and accuracy; our findings are presented in greater detail in appendix II.

We also interviewed FAA and union officials representing major aviation employee groups about facility conditions. In addition, to observe conditions and to speak with knowledgeable staff to learn about any facility deficiencies and the projects for fixing them, we selected a non-probability sample of facilities supporting operations and administrative functions in each of FAA's three geographic service areas (see table 10). We also spoke with officials of the Technical Center by phone and obtained documents from them.

Table 10: FAA Facilities GAO Contacted

Eastern Service Area	
	FAA Headquarters
	William J. Hughes Technical Center
	Washington, D.C., En-route Center
Central Service Area	
	Mike Monroney Aeronautical Center
	A buquerque Flight Standards District Office (FSDO)
	A buquerque En-route Center
	A buquerque Terminal Radar and Approach Control (TRACON) and Tower
	Oklahoma City TRACON and Tower
Western Service Area	
	Long Beach FSDO
	Western Pacific Region Office
	Los Angeles En-route Center
	Los Angeles Tower
	Fullerton Tower (contract tower)
	Southern California TRACON

Source: GAO analysis.

To determine the most common types of workplace injuries and illnesses FAA employees have reported, if any, we reviewed FAA and Department of Labor (Labor) workers' compensation data from 2007 through 2012.[3] To assess the reliability of the data we (1) reviewed existing documentation about the data, (2) interviewed agency officials knowledgeable about the data, and (3) performed electronic testing of the data for obvious errors in accuracy and completeness. We found the data to be sufficiently reliable for the purposes of this report. Because of the variability of factors contributing to causing reported injuries and illnesses, our study does not attempt to link workers compensation claims to facility conditions.

---

[3] These data describe any claims submitted by employees for either (1) traumatic injury or (2) occupational disease or illness. In this report, we generally refer to these as claims for injuries and illnesses.

To determine the extent to which FAA responded to safety deficiencies identified through its inspections and those conducted by the Occupational Safety and Health Administration (OSHA), we interviewed FAA and OSHA officials as well as reviewed FAA and OSHA documents regarding this issue.

To determine the extent actions taken by FAA to ensure that its facilities are in good condition are consistent with leading practices for capital-investment decisions, we reviewed FAA's Capital Investment Plan's budget data (both actual and projected) for facility modernization and replacement, from 2008 through 2017. We also reviewed FAA's process for making capital-investment decisions and compared it to GAO's and Office of Management and Budget's leading practices. We also interviewed FAA officials on their reorganization efforts and reviewed documents on FAA's facility project prioritization schemes.

We conducted this performance audit from July 2012 to September 2013 in accordance with generally accepted government auditing standards. Those standards require that we plan and perform the audit to obtain sufficient, appropriate evidence to provide a reasonable basis for our findings and conclusions based on our audit objectives. We believe that the evidence obtained provides a reasonable basis for our findings and conclusions based on our audit objectives.

Appendix II: Assessment of FAA's Statistical Model to Estimate the Condition of Terminal Facilities

FAA estimates the condition of many terminal facilities using a statistical model developed by a technical-consulting firm. The model estimates the condition of facilities that have not been physically inspected in the past 6 years, using data on the age and condition of facilities that have been inspected within that time period. The contractor has recommended that FAA revise its statistical models. In the 2012 roll-up report, the contractor notes that the baseline model is "preliminary and additional samples and adjustments to the formulas are needed for the results to be statistically valid." In this appendix, we describe our replication of the FAA model, using data from the agency's roll-up reports on facility condition, and assess the model's statistical precision. In addition, we discuss several alternative models we considered and their precision relative to FAA's baseline model.

FAA Model Estimates Terminal Facility Condition with Substantial Imprecision

FAA uses a combination of direct inspection, assumptions about the decline of a facility's condition within 6 years of inspection, and statistical methods to estimate the condition of terminal facilities. For facilities that have been inspected in a given year, FAA uses the results of those inspections to estimate facility condition in that year. Over the next 5 years, FAA plans to update the condition of the facility from the baseline of its direct inspection, using a formula that incorporates assumptions about expected deterioration. After 6 years have elapsed since the inspection, FAA uses statistical methods to estimate facility condition.

The specific statistical method that FAA uses for these less recently inspected facilities is a regression model that predicts facility condition—either the Facility Condition Index (FCI)[1] or deferred maintenance measured in dollars—as a function of facility age. Specifically, the model assumes that the unknown condition of a facility i is

$$y_i = \mathrm{E}(y_i \mid age_i) = \alpha + \beta age_i,$$

,

with the intercept α fixed at 100 in the model of FCI and 0 in the model of deferred maintenance. FAA's contractor fits the model to data on condition and facility age for facilities inspected within the past 6 years.

---

[1] The FCI is equal to 100 - deferred maintenance / facility value. FAA has reported FCI as a percentage, but this scaling choice does not affect the analysis here.

Appendix II: Assessment of FAA's Statistical
Model to Estimate the Condition of Terminal
Facilities

These inspection data estimate β and, thus, the unknown condition of facilities that were not inspected recently. In the 2012 roll-up report, FAA reports that $\hat{\beta}$ = -0.203 for the model of FCI and $\hat{\beta}$ = \$12,668 for the model of deferred maintenance. Since the model requires FCI and deferred maintenance to equal zero when age equals to zero, the model predicts a facility's condition using its age alone. For example, the 2012 model would predict that all 10 year-old facilities have a FCI of 98.0 and deferred maintenance of \$126,680, regardless of any other characteristics that could vary across the facilities.

All statistical estimates, including FAA's predictions of facility condition, have estimation error associated with them. In this application, we are specifically interested in the prediction error of FAA's model—that is, the amount by which FAA's condition estimates for uninspected facilities can be expected to vary from the true condition that would be measured in new physical inspections. We can model this prediction error for each facility as

$$e_i = y_i - \hat{y}_i = y_i - \hat{\beta} age_i \,,$$

which implies that

$$y_i = \hat{\beta} age_i + e_i \,.$$

Statistical models of the type that FAA uses to estimate facility condition typically assume that the error of prediction, e_i, varies randomly, such that $E(e_i) = 0$ and $Var(e_i) = \sigma^2$. If one applies this assumption to FAA's model, the expected amount by which a new physical inspection of a facility with a fixed age would vary from FAA's estimate is given by

$$Var(y_i) = Var(\hat{y} + e_i) = Var(\hat{y}) + \sigma^2 \,. [2]$$

The expected error of a new inspection, given the FAA model's prediction, is equal to the variance of the predicted value, which depends on the size of the sample used to estimate β and facility age, plus a term

---

[2] See Jeffrey M. Wooldridge, *Introductory Econometrics: a Modern Approach*, 2nd ed. Mason, OH: Thomas South-Western, pp. 203-206.

Appendix II: Assessment of FAA's Statistical
Model to Estimate the Condition of Terminal
Facilities

σ^2 measuring the variance of y around its mean for the population of facilities at a fixed age.[3]

In order to assess the precision of the FAA model estimates, we assembled data on facility age and the results of physical inspections from the 2010 through 2012 roll-up reports. For the 2010 sample, we assumed that all inspections which FAA defined as "actual" provided new data for analysis, even though many facilities were not physically inspected in 2010 but, instead, had values that were updated from an inspection conducted within the prior 6 years. This assumption was reasonable for our analysis, because 2010 was the first year in which the inspections were available to analyze. For the 2011-2012 sample, we treated inspections as providing new data only if they were conducted in those years. FAA considered inspections within 6 years of 2011 or 2012 to have provided "actual" data on condition for the purpose of model estimation, but in practice, these data were mathematically adjusted from prior years. From a statistical perspective, these data are not new observations, because FAA only measured condition once, in the year the inspection occurred.[4]

We fit the FAA model to the 2010 sample of 114 facilities in order to replicate the estimates from the roll-up reports and assess their precision. The 2010 sample allowed us to assess the fit of the model on the same data used to estimate its parameters, also known as the "in-sample" fit. Using the model fitted to the 2010 sample, we predicted the condition of 33 facilities that were physically inspected in either the 2011 or 2012 samples. By comparing the condition predicted by the model to the actual condition measured in physical inspections, we estimated the model's "out-of-sample" predictive power for new, unknown data. Evaluating a model's ability to predict beyond the sample of data used to develop it helps avoid placing too much emphasis on random features of any one sample that can influence the model's estimates. Moreover, the purpose of FAA's model is to predict unknown facility conditions.

---

[3]This assumes that the population process generating the data used to estimate the model does not change between the time the model was estimated and the collection of new data.

[4]More technically, these data could not have been new, random draws from a population data generation process, because they were calculated using a fixed mathematical formula. Our sample contrasts with the data FAA's contractor uses to estimate the parameters of its prediction model, which uses data from all inspections conducted in the last 6 years.

Appendix II: Assessment of FAA's Statistical
Model to Estimate the Condition of Terminal
Facilities

Table 11 shows the results of our analysis, and figure 3 graphically depicts the 2010 data and model fit. We summarized the predictive accuracy of the FAA model using various statistics, in part due to the skewed distribution of FCI and deferred maintenance. Our estimated values of β— -0.227 on the FCI scale and $14,565 on the deferred maintenance scale—were similar to the values FAA reported in its 2010 roll-up report (-0.225 and $12,551). However, our replication confirmed the contractor's assessment that the FAA model does not predict facility condition with a high degree of precision. On the FCI scale, the root mean squared error (RMSE) of prediction—which is similar to the estimated variance of prediction error also reported in table 11—was 3.4 in the 2010 sample used to estimate the model and 3.9 in the 2011-2012 validation sample. On the deferred maintenance scale, the RMSE was $606,862 in the estimation sample and $370,875 in the validation sample. The sample variance of FCI and deferred maintenance helps put the size of these results into context. In the estimation sample, the standard deviation was 5.0 and the middle 50 percent of the FCI distribution ranged from 90.9 to 96.6. The middle 50 percent of the deferred maintenance distribution ranged from $231,420 to $663,944, with a standard deviation of $565,421. These statistics are consistent with the large confidence intervals of prediction in figure 3. For example, the deferred-maintenance predictions for 10 and 40 year-old facilities have 95 percent confidence intervals ranging from 0 to $1,353,723 and from 0 to $1,797,599, respectively.[5] Together, these results show that FAA's estimates of facility condition vary meaningfully from the results of physical inspections.

---

[5]The confidence intervals are truncated at zero, because the deferred maintenance and FCI must be non-negative.

Appendix II: Assessment of FAA's Statistical
Model to Estimate the Condition of Terminal
Facilities

Table 11: Results of Replication and Predictive Validation of FAA Model

	Facility Condition Index (0-100)		Deferred Maintenance (dollars)	
	2010 Sample (estimation and prediction)	2011-2012 Sample (prediction only)	2010 Sample (estimation and prediction)	2011-2012 Sample (prediction only)
Parameters				
ß	-0.227	NA	14,565	NA
σ	3.392	NA	609,500	NA
Fit statistics				
Root mean squared error	3.377	3.869	606,862	370,875
Root median squared error	1.524	1.823	217,415	221,592
Mean absolute error	2.371	2.690	343,660	280,211
Median absolute error	1.524	1.823	217,400	221,592
Total error	NA	NA	13,255,775	-2,417,559
Total absolute error	NA	NA	39,177,277	9,246,953
N	114	33	114	33

Source: GAO analysis of FAA roll-up report data.

Note: Entries in the "2010 sample" columns are estimates from a FAA statistical model of facility condition fit to data from the agency's 2010 roll-up report on this topic. We used the estimated model to predict the condition of facilities that were physically inspected in 2011 or 2012. Entries in the "2011-2012" sample columns are statistics summarizing the predictive accuracy of the 2010 model on these later data.

Appendix II: Assessment of FAA's Statistical
Model to Estimate the Condition of Terminal
Facilities

Figure 3: Estimated versus Actual Deferred Maintenance in 2010

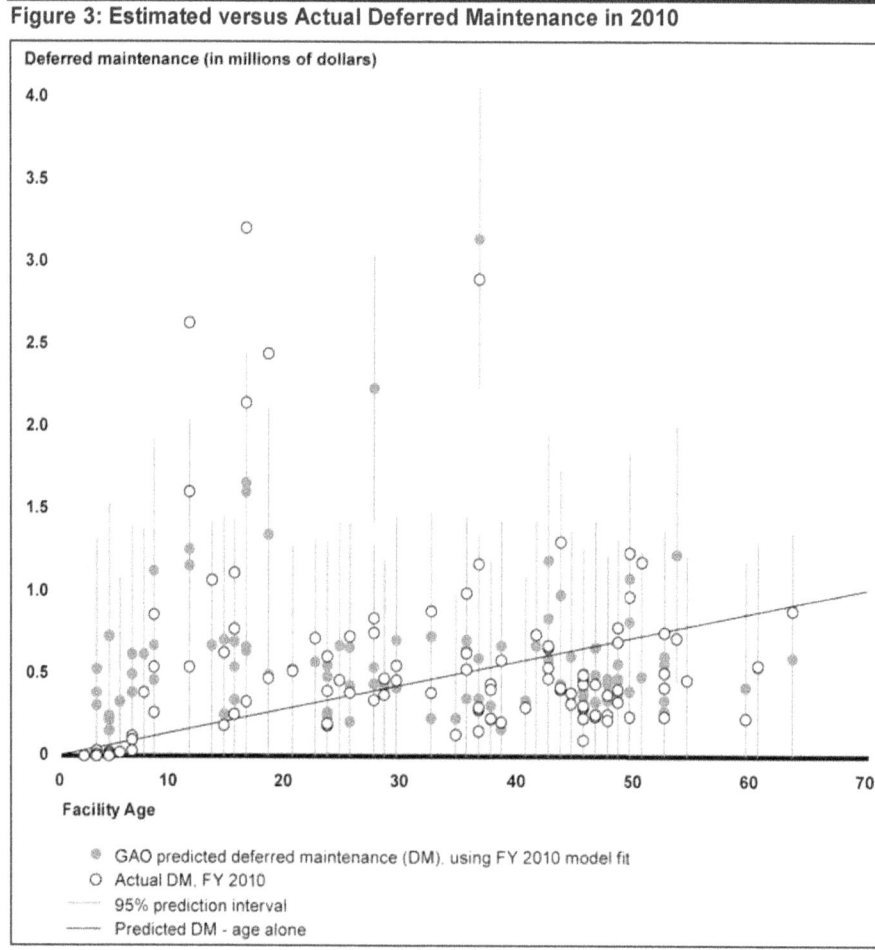

Source: GAO analysis of FAA terminal facility data.

Alternative Methods Can Improve the Precision of Some Facility Condition Estimates

Given the imprecision of FAA's model, we analyzed data available from the agency's roll-up reports to assess whether alternative methods could predict terminal facility condition more accurately. We measured the following variables for the same facilities and time periods described above: facility size (square footage); geographic location, including the facility's latitude and longitude; architectural design type; class of facility by function, such as whether a facility was a "tower with radar" or "combined TRACON and tower;" and whether FAA maintained and/or owned the facility (respectively). To measure facility value, we calculated the value implied by FAA's data on FCI and deferred maintenance.

Appendix II: Assessment of FAA's Statistical
Model to Estimate the Condition of Terminal
Facilities

We used several approaches to systematically search for alternative prediction methods, collectively known as "data mining" techniques. As with our evaluation of the baseline FAA model, we used the 2010 sample for estimating and comparing models and the 2011-2012 sample for validating the predictions on new data. We would have preferred to divide the available data into three parts to estimate, refine, and test alternative models, as recommended by methodological guidance on data mining. The small sample size precluded this approach, however.

Our first approach involved estimating a series of linear regression models that added various combinations of the variables above as predictors to the baseline FAA model. This "stepwise" search produced a model that minimized the Akaike Information Criterion (AIC), which is closely related to the residual sum of squares and R-squared statistics for the type of linear Normal models used by FAA. This procedure did not identify a more predictive model than the baseline FAA model, but it did identify a more predictive model of deferred maintenance:

$$E(DM_i \mid x_i) = \beta_1 age_i + \beta_2 value_i + \beta_3 age_i \cdot value_i + design_i \delta + class_i \theta + owner_i \gamma$$

(GAO Model D1)

Our second approach used recursive partitioning or "tree" methods to predict facility condition. This approach placed facilities into groups defined by the covariates, and then estimated condition as the mean within each group. Various classifications of facilities into covariate groups were searched to minimize the Akaike Information Criterion, which implicitly considered interactions and non-linearities among the covariates. In this sense, a recursive partitioning search complemented our application of stepwise methods, which assumed that all variables had linear relationships and no interactions (except for latitude and longitude). The clustering, non-linearity, and skewness in the distribution of facility condition (see fig. 3) makes these assumptions somewhat unrealistic. Fitting a constant value for each group may be more appropriate, given these features of the data. Partitioning methods require "pruning," a process in which covariate groups of various sizes are searched to minimize the bias (average error) of the predictions while controlling their variance. We chose the pruning parameter that minimized the mean prediction error over 10 cross-validated samples of the 2010

Appendix II: Assessment of FAA's Statistical
Model to Estimate the Condition of Terminal
Facilities

data.[6] The final tree implied the following piecewise constant regression models for FCI and deferred maintenance:

$$\mathrm{E}(FCI_i \mid x_i) = \beta_0 + \beta_1 I(9.5 \leq age_i < 24.5) +$$
$$\beta_2 I(24.5 \leq age_i < 47.5, latitude_i \geq 30.46) +$$
$$\beta_3 I(24.5 \leq age_i < 47.5, latitude_i < 30.46) + \beta_4 I(age_i > 47.5)$$
(GAO Model F1)

$$\mathrm{E}(DM_i \mid x_i) = \beta_0 + \beta_1 I(TRACON_i = 0, age_i < 6.5) +$$
$$\beta_2 I(TRACON_i = 0, age_i \geq 6.5, value_i < 4{,}275{,}383) +$$
$$\beta_3 I(TRACON_i = 0, 6.5 \leq age_i < 47.5, 4{,}275{,}383 \leq value_i < 7{,}381{,}382) +$$
$$\beta_4 I(TRACON_i = 0, age_i \geq 47.5, 4{,}275{,}383 \leq value_i < 7{,}381{,}382)$$
$$\beta_5 I(TRACON_i = 0, 6.5 \leq age_i < 30.5, value_i \geq 7{,}381{,}382) +$$
$$\beta_6 I(TRACON_i = 0, age_i \geq 30.5, value_i \geq 7{,}381{,}382)$$
(GAO Model D2),

where $I(.)$ is the indicator function and $TRACON_i$ equals 1 if the architectural design was a "Large TRACON" and 0 otherwise. Note that the intercept estimates the mean for large TRACONs. Fitting separate values according to whether the facility is a large TRACON is consistent with the data in figure 3, which shows that this class of facility often produces large outliers with respect to the mean value conditional on age and with respect to the marginal distribution of facility value.[7] In addition, constant fits may better estimate the condition of very young facilities, which cluster toward a FCI of 100 and deferred maintenance of $0.

In addition to searching broadly over the available data to improve prediction, we developed a model that simply adjusted the FAA baseline approach to predicting deferred maintenance by incorporating the facility's value (calculated as the cost of facility replacement):

---

[6]Trevor Hastie, Robert Tibshirani, and Jerome Friedman, *The Elements of Statistical Learning* (New York: Springer-Verlag, 2001) discusses cross-validation and pruning for recursive partitioning methods in more detail.

[7]A similar version of the tree model of deferred maintenance is a three-way interaction of age, facility value, and an indicator for whether the facility was a large TRACON. The out-of-sample RMSE of the three-way interaction model was $272,169, compared to $263,292 for the tree model. Alternatively, one could estimate a model with the two-way interaction of age and value separately for large TRACONs and all other facilities.

Appendix II: Assessment of FAA's Statistical
Model to Estimate the Condition of Terminal
Facilities

$$\mathrm{E}(DM_i \mid x_i) = \beta_1 age_i + \beta_2 value_i + \beta_3 age_i \cdot value_i$$

(GAO Model D3)

This model makes the effects of age and value conditional on the other variable, so that deferred maintenance can vary across facilities of the same age. In contrast, the baseline FAA model assumes that all facilities of the same age have the same deferred maintenance, which ignores the fact that facilities of the same age vary widely in value and, thus, deferred maintenance.

As shown in table 12, our alternative models predicted deferred maintenance more precisely than FAA's baseline model. On the deferred maintenance scale, our models improved the RMSE of deferred maintenance by at least $234,385 (39 percent) in the 2010 estimation sample and by $118,065 (32 percent) in the 2011-2012 validation sample. When assessed on other fit statistics, our models of deferred maintenance typically outperform FAA's baseline. The difference is largely due to the fact that our models incorporate facility value when predicting deferred maintenance, which should explain a large proportion of the variation across facilities of varying size. In contrast, we were unable to substantially improve FAA's model of FCI. The RMSE of our tree-selected model was 8.6 percent smaller than that of the FAA baseline in the 2010 sample, but the fit statistics did not consistently favor either model in the new 2011-2012 sample. FAA might prefer one model or another on these measures of fit, according to the goals of prediction. For example, if FAA sought to minimize to the error of the estimated total deferred maintenance, the total error or total absolute error would be appropriate measures of prediction accuracy.

Appendix II: Assessment of FAA's Statistical
Model to Estimate the Condition of Terminal
Facilities

Table 12: Results of Replication and Predictive Validation of FAA Model

	Root mean squared error	Root median squared error	Mean absolute error	Median absolute error	Total error	Total absolute error
FCI (0-100)						
2010 Sample						
FAA baseline	3.377	1.524	2.371	1.524	NA	NA
GAO model F1	3.088	1.519	2.177	1.519	NA	NA
2011-2012 Sample						
FAA baseline	3.869	1.823	2.690	1.823	NA	NA
GAO model F1	4.221	1.663	3.143	1.663	NA	NA
Deferred Maintenance (dollars)						
2010 Sample						
FAA model,	606,862	217,415	343,660	217,400	13,255,775	39,177,277
GAO model D1	288,431	138,714	195,861	138,713	0	21,152,937
GAO model D2	303,155	99,441	175,479	99,438	0	20,004,600
GAO model D3	372,477	156,211	238,010	156,205	-1,106,601	25,705,067
2011-2012 Sample						
FAA model	370,875	221,592	280,211	221,592	-2,417,559	9,246,953
GAO model D1	294,992	244,965	232,250	244,965	-1,802,472	6,270,737
GAO model D2	263,292	126,139	187,338	126,102	-608,089	5,994,801
GAO model D3	252,810	157,797	187,201	157,797	-810,940	5,054,426

Source: GAO analysis of FAA roll-up report data.

Note: Entries are fit statistics of statistical models developed on a sample of 114 facilities from the 2010 FAA roll-up report. Results for the 2010 sample are the in-sample fit statistics, while results for the 2011-2012 sample are out-of-sample fit statistics.

Implications for Revising Prediction Models

Our analysis suggests that data available to FAA would allow the agency to substantially improve its model of deferred maintenance. Specifically, incorporating facility value along with age and perhaps facility class and architectural design type would better exploit the available data. Additional revisions also may be appropriate, depending on the available data. FAA could refine the mathematical form of the model over time, as new inspections are conducted to provide additional data for model validation.

Appendix II: Assessment of FAA's Statistical
Model to Estimate the Condition of Terminal
Facilities

Although we were unable to improve upon FAA's model of FCI, the best available model still does not predict FCI with a high degree of precision. Additional data beyond the variables available to us in the roll-up reports may help identify a more predictive model. For example, data on typical weather conditions, usage, or building materials may improve predictions of FCI beyond what is possible using the variables we considered here and FAA's consultant has considered previously. If these data are available and are correlated with condition and if their collection and analysis costs less than the error caused by FAA's baseline model, incorporating additional variables could be a cost-effective solution to estimating FCI for facilities that have not been physically inspected in recent years.

Our findings are consistent with those of FAA's consultant, which has recommended that FAA revise its statistical models. In its 2012 roll-up report, the consultant notes that the baseline model is "preliminary and additional samples and adjustments to the formulas are needed for the results to be statistically valid." They recommended addressing outliers in the distribution of facilities and including additional predictors of facility condition.[8] In a 2008 report, the contractor recommended adjusting the physical inspection process to ensure a representative sample is available for statistical analysis.[9] The latter recommendation could be implemented as an inspection plan that selects facilities according to known probabilities, which would ensure that estimates of facility condition are unbiased and have known sampling variances. The sample could be designed in such a way to incorporate known maintenance problems or inspection needs, such as by selecting facilities for inspection with unequal probabilities from within strata defined by age, size, or other important variables. A probability sample could be particularly useful for reporting average or total condition across facilities.

---

[8]Jacobs Engineering, "Organizational 2012 Final MARS Roll-Up Report for 128 ATCT-TRACON Sites (January 2007 – December 2012)," January 2013, pp. 24-26.

[9]Jacobs Engineering, "Organizational Roll-Up Report for 109 ATCT – TRACON Sites," November 2008, Appendix C, pp. 2, 5.

Appendix III: GAO Contact and Staff Acknowledgments

GAO Contact	Gerald L. Dillingham, Ph.D., (202) 512-2834, or dillinghamg@gao.gov
Staff Acknowledgments	In addition to the individual named above, GAO staff who made key contributions to this report are Michael Armes, Assistant Director; Martha Chow; Colin Fallon; James Geibel; Kathleen Gilhooly; Daniel Hoy; Grant Mallie; SaraAnn Moessbauer; and Jeff Tessin.